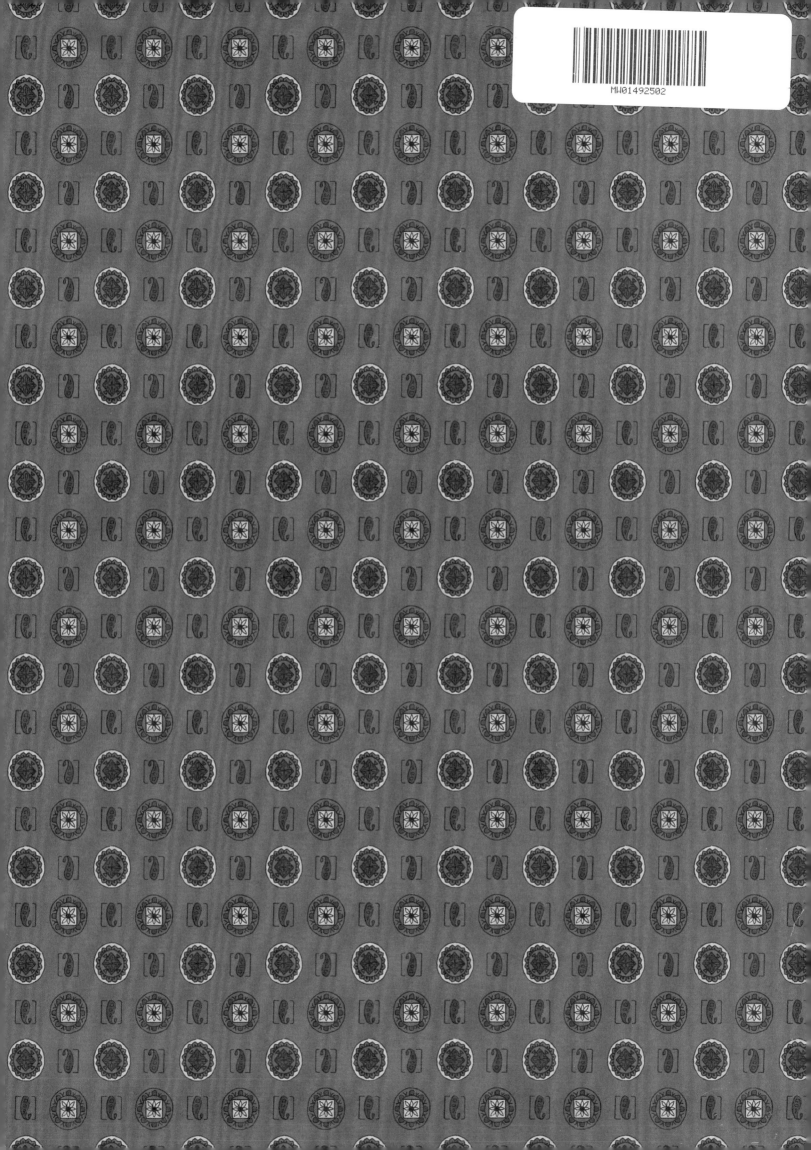

Golden Light

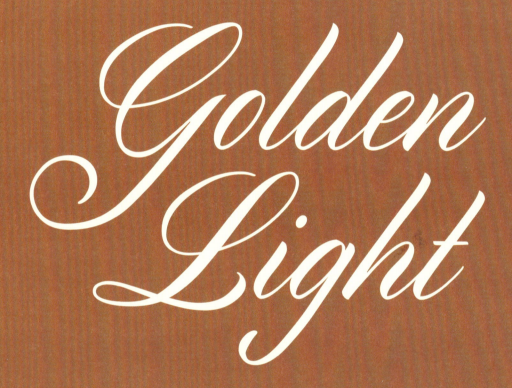

Golden Light

THE INTERIOR DESIGN OF NICKEY KEHOE

Principal Photography by Roger Davies

RIZZOLI
NEW YORK

New York · Paris · London · Milan

ON THE COVER The entry foyer of the Griffith Park Hills house.
PREVIOUS PAGE A light well in a monastery in Arles, France, provided
inspiration that informed the design of the Griffith Park Hills house.

FOREWORD

Liz Lambert

The book you are holding in your hands is the first monograph on Nickey Kehoe, introducing their work to the world at large, out of the shop and into the streets, out of the places where people live and onto these pages. Let them inspire you the way they have inspired me. Nickey Kehoe helped me make my house a home.

My company creates hotels. We conceptualize, design, and oversee the day-to-day operations of an assortment of places, from high camp to decadent luxury, from beachfront bungalows in Baja to trailers and tepees in the desert of far west Texas. Daily we strive to make the people who visit our hotels feel organically at ease, amused, and delighted, engaged in the colors, textures, and story of a place, more grounded, more whole. It's work to design the details of an immersive experience, and it takes a village to pull it off properly.

A few years ago, my wife and I bought an old house in Laurel Canyon, a little bungalow with good bones and a certain humility. We took the first steps of a renovation to reveal the white plaster walls, big wooden rafters, and a perfect little brick fireplace, and then we created a kitchen made of oak. But the kitchen needed dishes and glasses and napkins, and the plaster walls needed a painting or two or three. The outdoor deck needed a big farm table and chairs for friends to gather, and a vase to fill with flowers to set in the center of the table. We needed warmth and emotion.

The last thing either of us had that fall was the time to scour flea markets for the perfect find, or go shop to shop for the stuff we needed. Our usual fellow villagers were otherwise occupied by more pressing matters; however, one of them suggested I check out Nickey Kehoe's shop on Beverly. Down the hill and over the flats I tumbled, for the first time, into that bohemian treasure trove of rustic, modern, chromed, Craftsman, mid-century, handmade, reclaimed, and custom collection of furniture and art. For the first time, I took in the Turkish rugs, Danish leather chairs, delicately woven baskets, ceramic pendants hung with big brass hoops, cast bronze fixtures designed by Nickey Kehoe in conjunction with Urban Electric, and the rest of the menagerie that defines the aesthetic of Todd Nickey and Amy Kehoe.

Who are these hunter-gatherers who have curated this collection of patina and texture while producing such a beautiful family of original furniture to boot, I wondered? What is that metal blue Bauhaus sling chair sitting atop a table I see—is it a sculpture? Can you actually sit in it? Hard to say. But it's pleasant, the glaze of the paint, the wear on the original canvas sling, the curve of the metal tubing—like a tripod, the awkward charm of its stance! Distressed, imperfect? No matter. I saw that they understood what it means to repair what exists.

Here are some of the treasures I have taken home from the shop in the two years since that first visit: a stack of plates of cobalt honey-comb-glazed terra-cotta, now nestled on the shelf next to six Italian pasta bowls swirled and splattered with gentle green; a dark and moody brutalist painting, heavily layered with blacks and browns and cream; piles of indigo-dyed and patterned pillows, stuffed with soft but hefty feathers; an oversize, unglazed earthen table lamp that looks like what would have happened if Jackson Pollock had made pottery; an original Nickey Kehoe wide-plank, sun-bleached harvest dining table (of high character and minimal language) surrounded by a family of original Nickey Kehoe iron chairs, cast to look like their wooden Windsor sisters, but with all subtle imperfection intact in the mold, in the most *wabi-sabi* of ways.

I'm talking about small things here, about particular found and invented pieces of furniture, of *objets* and art, but taken as a whole, they form a point of view. An attitude of warmth and casual sophistication. Unforced. It says: repair what exists. It is a love for the natural that I find is so often missing from design. This attitude is carried into the interior design in the pages to follow, from the irreverence of a wall painted deep banana to the natural ease and elegance of an overgrown garden wall.

Here's to making people feel grounded and good and free.
Here's to Nickey Kehoe.

A CURIOUS WORKSHOP

Todd Nickey and Amy Kehoe

I've learned that people will forget what you said, people will forget what you did, but people will never forget how you made them feel.

— Maya Angelou

When designing homes and spaces, we seek not just a look but a feeling. We are uncommonly sensitive to the ways in which a space can elevate the senses, enhance memories, and become not merely a set piece but a main character in the story of our clients' lives.

We are deeply connected to our work. As we must be. Creating the tactile, multi-textural, curiously imperfect spaces that compose a client's home requires going far beneath the surface. After all, a home is where meals are made, friends are welcomed, and fetes, whether impromptu or Gatsbyesque, are thrown—and where moments of desperately needed rest and respite occur.

We are inspired by the everyday and the extraordinary. Our curiosity knows very few bounds. The minor elements and small details that may seem secondary are, in our eyes, vital parts of a thriving whole that reflects the subtle rhythms of our clients' sensibilities. We are grateful for our projects and our clients who allow us to collaborate, let loose our curiosity, and create authentic narratives.

Within our design studio, we follow our own house codes.

First, we are lovers of simplicity, without fear of flair.
Our approach ranges from minimal to maximal, quiet to baroque, but the real grandeur is in that ephemeral feeling that a space evokes. We're fascinated by how a room can come together to express its own persona. We love keeping things simple, as though the design "just happened."

We are object-obsessed observers, paying keen attention to a client's passions, preferences, and beloved pieces, juxtaposing divergent shapes and styles in deceptively simple ways. So, while it appears a personal collection has been randomly put together, in fact this is the result of our mindful curation.

Second, we seek equilibrium and enchantment, a wink and a nod.
Each project begins with the process of determining how our clients define beauty, good design, sophistication, fun, solace. What draws them in, quickens their pulse. Then we seek to achieve equilibrium: Elegant but never staid. Proud but humble. Full of detail but rife with negative space.

The "wink" comes from the unexpected—a combination of layered patterns and palettes, mixing up time periods, a humorous gesture, clever lighting—any element that keeps our balance from becoming too predictable or formulaic.

We believe in a sanctuary from chaos, rooms that are grounding.
We believe that living spaces should heighten awareness to your state (ideally calm, restful, inspired). The rooms, kitchens, lounging areas, hallways, and doorways should be both launch and landing pads to a client's busy life. Part of this approach is ensuring that spaces have a place for the eye to rest, that too much doesn't happen all at once. Energy needs to breathe, or a space can become either frenzied or static. We see every space as a sanctuary waiting to happen.

We are fanciful not fancy.
While we love a little schmanse here and there, each piece in every space we design must have a story or a patina, whether literal or metaphorical. A sense that it was acquired, not purchased. Pieces that inspire curiosity, yet signal a sense of belonging. Our most important litmus test: it must fit in, and never stand out.

We are hunters and gatherers of your story.
The intimate collaboration between Nickey Kehoe design studio and our clients allows us to find the narrative that runs through our clients' homes. Of course, any discerning client can design and decorate their own home, but having a partner in the process is an exponential help. Not just in making decisions of what and where, but why . . . or why not.

There are countless routes to take, a million tiny decisions, even after a solid design narrative has been established. As business partners, we often find ourselves at a roadblock in our own homes—needing each other's input in order to get to the next step. In this way, we truly practice what we preach.

We are a curious workshop.
We begin projects not really knowing where the design is going to end, and that's what is most exciting to us. Along the way, we discover new depths to a client's taste, or unearth a great piece that becomes a focal inspiration for a room. We play with color and light, and, while assembling the items we love, find a true voice for our projects.

We are insatiably curious throughout the process, and we bring this philosophy to the development of our furniture and accessories as well.

Two decades ago, at one fateful dinner party in New York City, two young design-obsessed urbanites met. Amid the raucous conversation, they discovered both were on a parallel mission—a passion for shaping space, a humanity within design. And our story began.

Our partnership is in many ways like a nurtured home, built with inherent curiosity and a desire to hear the other's views, interpretations, humor, and wisdom. The "curious workshop" and our friendship are intertwined with our shared values of exploration, growth, patience, support, respect, and much laughter.

As we both say all the time, we could not do this single-handedly, nor would it be the studio that it is with a sole voice. This friendship is the lighthouse that guides us as we manage various projects, obstacles, and goals.

In 2003, the siren song of the West Coast grew louder and louder, until finally we heeded its call. Neither of us had roots in Los Angeles, so we were thrilled to discover it together. L.A. was a blank slate. Everything seemed new: how people lived and worked and got around this vast city. It was all a beautiful, if sometimes perplexing, adventure.

Early visits to iconic buildings—the Ennis House by Frank Lloyd Wright, Tony Duquette's Dawnridge, the Eames House, the landmark Bradbury Building, and countless other architecturally significant structures— made the city's decorative landscape seem infinite.

We "cross town" so much in our daily lives that we wanted to capture what that meant to us, both inside and outside our clients' homes. There's so much to L.A. that we didn't expect to find here—so much more than the iconic references we grew up revering.

And we've stayed here, growing our business and expanding our understanding of the built and natural world around us. There's a certain type of light, from the overcast early mornings to midday's intense rays and that glimmering forever setting sun as dusk falls. It follows us—or perhaps we follow it—throughout our day. This collection of projects follows the path of that light, from Pasadena in the east to Malibu and beyond in the west. It is for the curious, the admiring, the ambitious. For lovers of studied but unfussy design. For those chasing the feeling of being surrounded by beautiful things with a story to tell. For those who follow a different kind of light.

Pasadena

Pasadena

The most difficult projects for us—as artists, decorators, however we choose to define ourselves—are usually our own. We spend our work lives creating spaces we love, relying upon a design sensibility that keenly registers what our clients love and ultimately come to call home.

But when faced with our own projects, when we become the curators of our own desires, the task becomes infinitely more complex. We find ourselves sliding away from being discerning design professionals to becoming something else entirely. A pilgrim first setting foot on foreign shores. A kindhearted intruder. An inheritor. An impostor.

My husband, Greg, and I moved to our current house in the spring of 2015. Not only was it three times the size of our previous home, it was Greg's grandparents' house from 1952 to 1972 and so carried with it the weight of history and deep sentiment. He came home from the hospital here as a baby. The echoes of his childhood, raucous holiday parties, long summer afternoons, rang through every room, every hidden corner.

As a decorator, I faced three major hurdles. First off, the size and scale. I've worked on houses much larger, but all of this space was for just us, and it was daunting. Secondly, all the money we had went "behind the walls." Plumbing, five new furnaces, all the electrical, and poof! There was nothing left for furniture, rugs, or even lighting. Finally, the doozy: the philosophical challenge of designing spaces for myself, my spouse, and his grandparents' legacy, rooms that could express the memory, joy, and human drama that inhabited the house in the past, and make room for our future.

Over the course of four and a half years, we've had our share of false starts, bright ideas that quickly burned out, and many, many pieces of furniture brought over and returned. There were days I'd come to work at the studio feeling as though I had no idea what I was doing as a decorator. I felt like a fake and a phony. Finally, my mask was off.

In these moments, my partner, Amy Kehoe, was such a comfort, listening and offering simple solutions, and reminding me that many of our projects through the years have been tremendously challenging. That every home comes with a history, a story to be told, reinvented, or gently revised. And that every step in the process is just that— a step. One that is ascended through patience, resilience, listening to your instincts, and a determination to see the job through.

And we always do.

In the end, Greg and I are settled in, and incomparably happy in this house. This house that is finally, at last, our home.

— Todd Nickey

PAGE 11 An Easter Egger named Phylis roams the back garden of the house, which was built in 1927 of poured-form concrete. She lays baby blue eggs. OPPOSITE In the living room, the graphic black-and-white painting by Robert Chuey dates from 1954, and the piano is a 1921 Chickering. The chair is a neoclassical find from an estate sale.

OPPOSITE The blue tile baseboard in the dining room is original to the house, as are the brick floors. An illustration by Jean Cocteau (1961) hangs above a white marble scuplture. ABOVE The living room features built-in shelving that holds carved wood busts of Haitian rulers Henri Christophe and Alexandre Pétion.

The dining room chairs by Nickey
Kehoe are upholstered in Gert
Voorjans Day & Night fabric.

ABOVE This outdoor space, originally a Juliet balcony added in the 1950s, is used for breakfast on a regular basis. OPPOSITE The tub, tile, and brick floors in the guest bath are all original to the house. The wallpaper is by Howe.

PAGE 22 Gumwood countertops stand out against the cabinetry in the pantry. PAGE 23 The hood is original to the house, and the light fixtures were added by Greg's grandmother in the 1960s. ABOVE The interior courtyard in the middle of the house is used as a shortcut between the bedrooms and the kitchen in the warmer months. We found the terra-cotta pineapple in the background in Mexico. OPPOSITE The living room bookcase dates from the time the house was built. A buying trip for the shop to the South of France yielded the Art Deco navy chairs. The black-and-white photograph is by Robert Parke Harrison, and the foreground painting by Robert Chuey. PAGE 27 A view into the master bathroom, with wallpaper by Sandberg, and paintings to the right of the doorway by Mary Maguire. The wood mobile is a vintage find from Palm Springs.

ABOVE, LEFT Coffee table still life. ABOVE, RIGHT The cozy maid's room
has been reconfigured into an office. OPPOSITE The designers transformed
a former guest bedroom into a closet/office. The orange cabinet hails from
their early days in New York, and the lithograph is by Robert Rauschenberg.
PAGE 30 Cabinet of curiosities: vases and objects collected over the years.
PAGE 31 An Italian ceramic lion lamp adorns a bedside table in the master
bedroom. PAGE 33 In the master bedroom the wallpaper is by Iksel and the
headboard and bedside lamps are vintage finds from Texas. Mr. Brown and
Hedy, rescued from the Pasadena Humane Society, are sitting on a bedcover
by Les Indiennes.

I choose the rooms that I live in with care,
The windows are small and the walls almost bare,
There's only one bed and there's only one prayer;
I listen all night for your step on the stair.

— Leonard Cohen

Griffith Park Hills

Griffith Park Hills

Los Angeles is at its most intriguing, its truest, when an amalgam of seemingly incompatible styles and influences join together to create something radically new. This conflagration of then and now, of classical restraint and on-the-pulse cultural expression, resonates deeply in the lore of the movie industry. But we find the juxtaposition most alluring within the city's architecture.

This Los Feliz home, built in the 1920s, is known as a "Storybook" house, a combination of English Tudor and French Normandy styles. Elegant nooks and fine examples of carved woodwork abound in this quiet abode, but the story is much more fantastically complicated than that.

You see, our clients are modernists.

This project presented a particular set of challenges: introducing modern approaches and clean lines and layers into a traditional home; using the honed craftsmanship of the original structure to inspire freshly conceived, open, and livable spaces; and respecting the elegance of the architecture while introducing the bold simplicity of contemporary design.

L.A. finds a way of dipping its brush in every palette, and every so often the result comes out absolutely timeless. For us and for our clients, the house in the Griffith Park Hills had a perfect storybook ending.

PAGE 36 A lamp by Marianna Kennedy in the den. Behind the lamp is a folk art wood sculpture of a cat. PAGE 37 Simple, well-made objects take pride of place in the dark wood den, including the table by George Nakashima and the porcelain Nymphenburg hare on the mantel. OPPOSITE The foyer's sweeping staircase rises from the original slate floors and is illuminated by a Jean de Merry pendant and features a dresser by Ico Parisi. PAGE 40 A brass-front cabinet from JF Chen stands out against paneled walls. PAGE 41 Dining room vignette: A vintage Josef Frank cabinet topped by striking Syrian jars rising toward the original plaster ceiling. A stack of Roland Rainer dining chairs makes it easy to accommodate extra guests.

PAGE 42 A graceful arched doorway provides a view into the formal living room with its vintage bentwood chair and Nickey Kehoe sconce over the piano. PAGE 43 Another view of the dining room, with Roland Rainer dining chairs around a mid-century table that features Ted Muehling iron candlesticks. ABOVE Nickey Kehoe Instagram of cutting tools. OPPOSITE An industrial worktable with a cast-iron base painted red serves as an island in the kitchen that also features workhorse double side-by-side sinks. PAGE 46 The terrace overlooking the rear yard reflects the house's combination of English Tudor and French Normandy styles. PAGE 47 A cozy platform bed nestles under a Noguchi paper pendant.

Los Feliz Hills

Los Feliz Hills

Joan Didion wrote, "It is easy to see the beginnings of things, and harder to see the ends" in her essay "Goodbye to All That."

This home and its clients were an instrumental part of our beginnings in L.A., maintaining a clear and strong place in our memory. The substantial house in the "Italianate" style of the 1920s was set into the hills of Los Feliz, on the east side of Los Angeles. Walking in, we felt like we'd stumbled on an abandoned romantic mansion. The scale and grandeur were exhilarating and overwhelming all at once. We arrived at sunset, and warm light suffused the sprawling space.

Walking into the rotunda, we stood beneath the giant dome, our voices bouncing and reverberating throughout the space. It seemed gorgeously lost in time, a hidden paradise up there in the hills.

We had no idea it would take three years to complete this home. However, those three years created a foundation for our work aesthetic and a guiding light for our design process. Throughout this project, we developed our appreciation for blending the traditional with the modern. Drawing on the work of Jean-Michel Frank, we were guided by a sense of clean, modern glamour. Our clients' incredible art collection, which would have lent gravitas to any space, certainly helped.

Our charge was to make this vast, formative home feel warm and comfortable within its majestic shell, and we hope our vision echoes still today.

PREVIOUS PAGES A focal point in the voluminous and light-filled living room, a work by Elliot Hundley hangs above the composer's grand piano. OPPOSITE Nickey Kehoe intentionally avoided window treatments in the dining room, where majestic beams and leaded glass windows anchor images from Nan Goldin's seminal series of photos, "The Ballad of Sexual Dependency."

ABOVE Vignette from the Nickey Kehoe Shop. OPPOSITE A favorite room in the house: classic and modern notes meet perfectly in our client's home office, where we gave equal attention to her work reading scripts and to her children's art.

OPPOSITE In the master bath, a custom-made onyx vanity sits elegantly in front of a customized mural composed of hand-painted Gracie Studio wallpaper. Paavo Tynell's floral motif pendant whimsically illuminates the room. ABOVE Linen-wrapped closet doors line the dressing room. A Jacques Adnet desk perches against the leaded glass windows.

Los Feliz

Los Feliz

Situated at the base of Griffith Park in Los Feliz, our clients' 1924 Mediterranean home has an undeniable romance. Scale and light provided a leading role in fostering this spirit, which resonates with endless laughter, joy, and creativity.

While this spirit was elevating, our goal was to create a sense of intimacy and welcoming for their family in what is a quite voluminous space. We subdivided the vast living room into "rooms within rooms" to shift the grandeur of the space into something that would draw people together: a reading area, a space for the grand piano, and a main seating area. We maintained the sense of majestic volume by selecting furnishings with low profiles, thus exaggerating the room's height while keeping the seating area intimate. We chose a large rug to live up to the enormous scale of the room.

The dining room is a little jewel box in the center of the house. It's a beautifully curved room lined with windows all around that are darkened by lush ferns crawling up the exterior walls. Here, you are engrossed in a botanical world, where a mustard-toned wallpaper fosters the dreamy, beyond-the-garden-wall atmosphere.

Our clients infused so much joy into the design process. The exterior represents their appreciation of the decorative and considered world of design. They hired Samantha Gore of The Yard to tackle the landscape design. Gore's boundless creativity culminated in a stunning custom terra-cotta backdrop for the pool, with a double-walled hedge discreetly lining the perimeter to create privacy. The entrance is a perfect assemblage of variously scaled pots and succulents, so other-worldly that you're already transported before you enter the house.

Designing homes is always an ongoing discussion. As our clients return to us for their second or third homes, it informs our process, and allows us to make more specific and holistic choices about what they need. The best interior design is never static, it grows and shifts, and traces the journey of the people who live within it. The greatest inspiration of all is creating spaces where people can live and flourish and tell their stories.

PREVIOUS PAGES Golden hues fill the generously scaled living room. An impressively large antique Oushak rug grounds the multiple seating groups. OPPOSITE Ornate crown molding wraps the family room walls, while an unfussy Nickey Kehoe string pendant and braided jute rug provide an earthy counter-balance. PAGE 64 Natalie Page pendants and a reclaimed wood island top imbue the spacious, light-filled kitchen with a sense of the tactile and handmade. PAGE 65 Pure grandeur in this breathtaking two-story entry: The romantic colonnade appears never-ending, as the largest of the Noguchi lanterns floats cloudlike, so as not to interfere with the architecture.

Inspired by the drama of the curved walls in the dining room, we kept going with a bold spirit, continuing with more golden hues in the Finnish wallpaper, Night of the Skylarks. ABOVE What could have been a pass-by area between bedrooms evolved into a library for this family of readers. Curved bookcases and window benches define the space with dark and plush finishes and textures. LEFT A playful entry: The ceramic owl sconce by Georges Pelletier and the client's own artwork casually welcome friends and family. OPPOSITE An antique rug and demilune table adorn the crisp colonnade of arches of the second floor landing area. FOLLOWING PAGES In the master bedroom, we created a calm mix of texture and color. The eye wanders, taking in individual elements—the plaster chandelier, cane bed, vintage bench—without a single piece vying for all the attention.

ABOVE Our young client's love of pink fit naturally with the original romantic crystal sconces, which she found glamorous and feminine. The big challenge for us was ample storage of all kinds—decorative hooks for costumes, pinboards for drawings, books—for her highly creative spirit. OPPOSITE, ABOVE For the then tween boy's room, embracing the collector's spirit led to the best compositions—hats hang above the bed in lieu of art. OPPOSITE, BELOW An embroidered style patch honoring the spirit of Nickey Kehoe. FOLLOWING PAGES A sweeping olive tree anchors the exterior. Wildly alive ferns wrap the curvature of the house, enchanting eyes both inside and out. A fading terra-cotta tile patio gives way to the more natural elements of decomposed granite underneath.

SEEK RISK
FIND ART
TRAVEL OFTEN

NICKEY KEHOE

Nickey Kehoe Early Years

A little Spanish duplex in Silver Lake was the first place we called home, after pulling up stakes in New York. We went as far west as we could, dipped our toes in the Pacific, and still ended up living on the East Side of Los Angeles. We each landed in Los Angeles, renting in various neighborhoods, testing the waters. Then, as luck or good partnership would have it, after a few years, we were separately looking for homes when Todd discovered a charming side-by-side duplex that sparked our design sensibility. We loved how the sunshine shimmered through the Douglas firs along Silver Lake Boulevard. The neighborhood offered both a quaint respite and an urban, walkable community that, as New Yorkers, we appreciated. The undulating curves, topsy-turvy-every-which-way streets, where you can tuck yourself into the hills and get lost in the best way, stirred our imaginations. Dotted with magical "secret" hillside stairways and bridges that connect its far-flung terraces, the neighborhood maintains a true sense of creativity and wonder, and it was a magical place for us to get settled and develop what would become Nickey Kehoe, as we call the house.

Todd met his future husband while we were living together here. He started rescuing dogs and fostering them here, and Amy's son, Wyeth, was born while we lived here. We both felt a tremendous sense of inspiration, of indelible possibility.

We call this our "the walls can speak" era—a time of being influenced by one another's efforts, consciously and happily helping each other explore our inspirations. We look back and often feel that a certain boldness was born out of this incubation period, from the deep teal of Todd's bedroom walls to the wide stripes down the narrow hallway on Amy's side. The house served as a wonderful sketch pad of ideas, a place where stories and designs could develop and thrive before we shared them with our clients and the world.

OPPOSITE Collection of inspiration: a hand-painted envelope from our longtime collaborator Sean Daly. Samples of product development and a nod to our past—Todd as a little boy on his beloved horse Hippy (named for his long 1970s hair). One of our custom tissue papers developed for the shop as well as snapshots of store vignettes.

BELOW Todd in his living room with its signature white floors, vintage mirror, and vintage Pfister for Knoll sofa. The sofa moved from his New York loft to Los Angeles and gained new life with a simple reupholstery.

BELOW Amy's living room with vintage Cleo Baldon chairs and golden waxed linen drapes. The drapes have since made two moves and continue to anchor the rooms they inhabit. Artwork by Celia Gerard, from Sears-Peyton Gallery.

OPPOSITE Collection of inspiration and memories: Amy as a little girl on her family's golden linen sofa—a precursor to the drapes. Nickey Kehoe's beloved neon sign on the shop's art deco building. A collection of note cards, designed and developed with Thunderwing Studio.

THE FUTURE IS BRIGHT

nickey · kehoe

OPPOSITE Collection of inspiration and memories. Photograph of Todd and Amy taken for *Domino* magazine circa 2005. Amy, age six, also on a pony, different location from Todd, yet same interests. Custom ribbed metal sample developed for product. Shot of the vintage salmon-painted shop doors, found in 2012 and recently installed in the new space.

BELOW Todd's dining room and a partial view of his kitchen. Many dinner parties occurred here as we formed new friendships in Los Angeles. Miguel Flore-Vianna captured this shot.

BELOW Amy's bedroom: The tufted headboard was the prototype for the Nickey Kehoe headboard—our homes proved to be trusty testing grounds. The bedding is by Matteo, and the trunk and table lamp are vintage.

OPPOSITE A collage of memories: A custom bag and floral tissue we made for the shop. Our "seek risk" patch was sent to clients and friends one holiday season. A shot of Amy's striped hallways and outtakes from our first shop on Highland Avenue, which opened in 2008.

OPPOSITE Collection of inspiration and memories: Todd and Amy on one of their first European buying trips. A vintage Portuguese tile found for a client's kitchen. Outtake of our first shop exterior. Early prototype of our NK hand sconce. Todd and his beloved dog Hedy in a photo shoot.

BELOW Todd's bedroom: The saturated teal walls and deep brown with hints of red trim around the windows. Vintage textiles grace his bed. Burlap drapes and seagrass floors lighten the rich tones—both have been tried-and-true materials utilized in many of our projects.

The Oaks

The Oaks

The Oaks are a hidden gem of a neighborhood in Los Angeles. Nestled between Beachwood Canyon and Los Feliz Hills, The Oaks refers to a hillside neighborhood with winding streets and hidden treasures at times parked on a cliff's edge.

Our clients' house has a modest single-story appearance from the street entrance. You're greeted by a beautiful foyer with strong, gestural Deco details that spill into the den, formal living room, and kitchen, which comprise the top floor. From every room there are sweeping views of the surrounding canyon. The two lower floors contain the bedrooms, an office, and a screening room.

Our challenge was to make this vertical living experience feel more kid-friendly for the young, growing family who would call it home. We opened up a few walls to create a seamless flow between rooms on the first floor. On the remaining floors, we simply modified surfaces and finishes and brought the house up to date.

The end result is a clean and cheerful home with lots of room to grow.

PREVIOUS PAGES We reconfigured the original dining room into a family room that connects to the breakfast area. The plaster details on the ceiling were restored. OPPOSITE We made the dining room/library table part of the living room, with a custom chandelier and bookcase by Nickey Kehoe. FOLLOWING PAGES A bank of windows in the master bedroom overlooks the canyon. The tufted headboard is Nickey Kehoe.

ABOVE, LEFT Nickey Kehoe Instagram featuring a book on kantha cloths and jewelry by Pascale Monvoisin. ABOVE, RIGHT The breakfast room connects to the family room. OPPOSITE Foyer detail: The floors, banister, and ceiling are all original. PAGE 98 Bathtub with a view to the canyon. PAGE 99 The casement-style shower features striking green Moroccan tile.

OPPOSITE Straw animal heads from France adorn the wallpaper of the nursery above the Jenny Lind–style crib. ABOVE Detail of the wallpaper and a sconce in the nursery. PAGE 103 In a guest bedroom a vintage headboard and floor lamps repose against William Morris wallpaper. PAGES 104 105 We took our inspiration for the screening room from RKO theaters.

Beachwood Canyon

Beachwood Canyon

There's something to be said for having a shop. A place separate from where you eat, sleep, argue, and relax, where you can flesh out ideas, and ultimately put them on display.

When you're immersed in such a space, that's when our designs and curation of objects really start to shine. People love that about our shop. We've had two locations since we settled in Los Angeles: the first, on Highland Avenue, and the current one, tucked into a sun-drenched stretch of Beverly Boulevard. Our clients in Beachwood fell in love with the Nickey Kehoe shop years ago, and the first time we went to see their home, it was like a time capsule of our store—a kind of living version of our favorite pieces, all in one space.

The home you see here once belonged to an artist, and the main living room served as the "atelier." The space needed quite a bit of love, and the clients, who were expecting their first child, gave us complete liberty to bring the house to life in seven months. The results were really spectacular—the kitchen floor is one of our all-time favorites—and the project was a triumph all around.

As the world of design enters the digital age, it's often those analog relationships, built with people who discover your work in the wild, that end up being the most meaningful and long-lasting.

PAGE 108 In the foyer the painted archway highlights the architecture. PAGE 109 Stairwell detail with rope banister. OPPOSITE A Nickey Kehoe headboard and vintage brass sconces from a French flea market pull together the master bedroom.

ABOVE, LEFT Vintage Dresser and vase. **ABOVE, RIGHT** NK Instagram.
OPPOSITE The plaster fireplace is a focus of the living room and is used
every day. **PAGES 114 115** We added Howe wallpaper to accentuate the
colors of the master bath, with its original tile work.

We converted the previous owners' painting studio into the living room, taking advantage of the double-height ceilings.

ABOVE NK Instagram. OPPOSITE
To make the kitchen more user-
friendly, we reorganized the layout
and added cement checkered tiles
for a punch of color.

Whitley Heights

Whitley Heights

We had the pleasure of designing a home in Whitley Heights, a coveted, historic enclave in the Hollywood Hills cherished for its 1920s charm and legacy. Through narrow, winding streets connected by flights of pedestrian stairs and original streetlamps, this little neighborhood takes you back to the origins of Hollywood living. Whitley Heights has a way of whisking you out of the hustle and bustle of the city and transporting you to somewhere otherworldly, and we wanted that magic to be part and parcel of this home

A number of actresses had called the house home before our client moved in. There is an undeniably creative, glamorously feminine spirit to the space. The house is filled with impractical whimsy, rooms disconnected from one another, and quirky bric-a-brac. We all agreed that these quirks were an essential part of the spirit of the space. These little eccentricities are better off embraced rather than masked or brushed aside. Celebrating the romance of the house, we dove into historic wallpapers, including witty, endearing William Morris rabbits, as well as vintage textiles and bedspreads.

There was no family room, rather a step-down, grand ballroom feel to the combined living and dining room. Our intention was to allude to the eras of literary salons and their hosts and allow for this large room to be the center of all gatherings, big or small, impromptu or impeccably orchestrated.

As it happens, our client started a family and moved on to a larger home. However, the next owners were taken with the home's unique and unclassifiable allure, thus continuing its legacy of romantic preservation.

PREVIOUS PAGES Crisp, clean white walls were offset by elegant forest green sateen wool drapes. The vintage rug and custom-made ottoman focus the room. OPPOSITE A William Morris wallpaper lining the entry and stairwell welcomes the outdoors in, creating an enchanting, gardenlike space. PAGE 126 Farrow & Ball wallpaper in the guest room pairs nicely with a vintage crochet bedspread. PAGE 127 The sitting room's walls are adorned with our client's collection of photographs— her great-great aunt was a famous silent film star. The vintage cabinet and French cane chairs provide a nice place to relax.

OPPOSITE Vintage rush chairs and brightly painted farm table in the breakfast room. **ABOVE** Pale blue walls and a custom armoire outfit the master bedroom. The loveseat is upholstered in a vintage kilim. **RIGHT** Nickey Kehoe Instagram with Astier de Villatte ceramics.

Outpost Estates

OPPOSITE The first move in the renovation was to sandblast the dark wood ceilings, exaggerating the indoor-outdoor lifestyle. ABOVE A shared bedroom for kids means that stuffed animals, dinosaurs, and other toys often seep into the adults' lives. Matching Jenny Lind beds and a shared nightstand, along with storage at the ends of the beds, help keep things tidy.

Outpost Estates

This house in Outpost Estates, in the Hollywood Hills, was another significant project that defined our studio early on—a sort of coming of age for Nickey Kehoe. A dear friend and her husband and family moved into this sprawling one-story home, and so much of the success of this home was due to our shared aesthetic vision. Our client was just as inspired by playing with whimsical vintage motifs and telling bold color stories as we are. The home is perfectly imperfect, with a look that captures the feeling of being decorated over time.

Shortly after we finished, the house was shot by *Domino* magazine. The response was positive and overwhelming. Our phone started to ring off the hook, and we found our voice connecting with an audience that has since grown into our tribe of clients, friends, and creative peers.

OPPOSITE The ease of dining alfresco just outside the living room doors. The dining table and chairs are all vintage. PAGE 136 The client's wood and Lucite desk/ vanity represents an homage to her femininity and modernity. PAGE 137 A vintage Arne Norell lounge chair and ottoman, Matteo linen bedding, and neutral kilim all speak to the relaxed, breezy master bedroom vibes.

Hancock Park No.1

Hancock Park No. 1

Hancock Park has a rarefied small-town sensibility in the middle of a great big city. This tree-lined neighborhood has always been a preferred hideaway for the Hollywood set. This Hancock Park house once belonged to Buster Keaton. Arguably, his most famous performance comes in 1928's *Steamboat Bill, Jr.*, when Keaton's character is admiring a build-it-yourself home he's just put together, and one of the walls comes crashing down around him. Lucky for us, his house in real life was far better built.

We designed this home for a large family—former New Yorkers like us—with four sons. When we started, the space had just been renovated, and we were working off a blank slate. The challenge here was to create a story for the house and give a narrative that would add depth and character to the architecture while still keeping it comfortable and approachable. At the same time, we needed to make sure the space could withstand the slapstick antics of a house full of boys. We like to think Buster Keaton would approve of the resulting mix of elegance and durability.

PREVIOUS PAGES The formal living room, with a Violetta marble fireplace designed by Nickey Kehoe, leads to the library. OPPOSITE We converted the former sunroom into a bar and entertainment space that extends into the outdoors.
FOLLOWING PAGES The family room looks over the lawn and pool area. Typical of houses of this era in Hancock Park, the maid's rooms were at the back of the house near the kitchen. This is probably the fifth renovation we have done in which we turned what was a maid's room into an open-plan kitchen/family room.

PAGE 146 The kitchen was inspired by a scullery kitchen. We decided on walnut counters for a warm palette. PAGE 147 Creeping fig covers the entry façade, which resembles a grotto. RIGHT The expansive master bedroom was formerly a large balcony.

PAGE 150 Nickey Kehoe Instagram Astier de Villatte teapots. PAGE 151 The elegant but informal mudroom separates the entertaining parts of the house from the private areas.

PAGES 152 153 The light-filled library connects the formal living room to the terrace. The ceiling, lacquered in Portola Paints "Peppersand," reflects the warm light at night. The mint green walls are a custom color by Portola.

Hancock Park No. 2

Hancock Park No. 2

Another one of our Hancock Park projects was a true labor of love. Or, in other words, a gut renovation.

This project included adding on a large master suite and excavating underneath the house to add a screening room and reroute the lower staircase.

Christine London added her magical yet measured landscaping gifts to the gardens, and the architecture firm JW Hilliard was brought on board, adding to the familiar and casually in-crowd nature of this incredible project.

One never knows which kind of spaces will inspire a sense of home, but in this case, despite months of tearing down and building up, planning and reshaping and reimagining, it was exactly as it should be. Theirs.

OPPOSITE The Italianate revival home was formerly owned by Buster Keaton and Natalie Talmadge. FOLLOWING PAGES The formal living room with a central seating plan provides an elegant yet slightly informal style for a young family. Robsjohn-Gibbings chairs, Hélène Aumont rope sconces, a custom coffee table ottoman with built-in tray, and pendants by Casamidy all contribute to the room's understated chic. PAGE 160 Delft plates decorate a wall covered in Gracie wallpaper above vintage Swedish demilune tables in the formal dining room. PAGE 161 NK Instagram.

PREVIOUS PAGES The custom dining table in the formal dining room seats twenty, with green leather chairs by Giannetti Home and wallpaper by Gracie. ABOVE The original stainless steel counter and the O'Keefe & Merritt stove (aka, O'grin and bear it stove). OPPOSITE The kids' bath has been updated, but the tub is original. FOLLOWING PAGES The pool and loggia are surrounded by evergreens and are anchored by a beautiful fireplace for chilly California evenings.

Wattles Park

Wattles Park

For us, the process of designing a home begins with a conversation. We speak with our client, often at length, before any physical work is done. This form of design therapy fosters a sense of trust on both sides, and takes on a particularly meaningful quality when your clients really know themselves and let you get to know them. It's that kind of clarity that inspires us to create the warm, intimate spaces we love so much.

This Spanish-style home in the Hollywood Hills is lovingly filled with music, art, artifacts, and animals, and the owners know what they like. This is the home of people who have earned their aesthetic point of view, and their space honestly reflects their journey. The house was dark yet still wonderfully welcoming when we first encountered it. One of our goals was to bring light to the space. It was important for us to introduce a few vibrant elements to open it up and reduce any sense of heaviness.

The great room, with its lofty ceiling, simply and elegantly calls people in, with a fireplace fender and jute rug that beg for intimate conversation. A cluster of guitars and a piano are constantly in use, and when our clients' son isn't playing, there's music pulsing through the speakers, encouraging conversation, candor, and connection.

We believe homes are meant to be lived in—in the present tense— a living, breathing space for expression as well as the unexpected, inexplicable wonders of daily life.

OPPOSITE Curvilinear stairs enclose layers of vintage tables, lighting, and art in the foyer. PAGE 172 With its impressive height, the living room is home to notable furnishings—a vintage Eames chair and ottoman, Robsjohn-Gibbings coffee table, and George Smith upholstery. PAGE 173 Artworks on the client's gallery wall range from family heirlooms to work by artist Cindy Sherman.

PREVIOUS PAGES A perfectly serene and humble kitchen. OPPOSITE Ready to slumber: A custom headboard and night-stands are illuminated by a vintage Scissor sconce with its original shade. LEFT A custom shelf was made to add decorative warmth to this perfectly intact 1930s bath. Crown molding in a graphic black line mimics the tile. PAGE 178 NK Instagram of Il Buco platters. PAGE 179 Not short on wit, the powder room serves as the home for the client's collection of chalk-ware faces and books.

Venice

Venice

Wherever you are in the city of Los Angeles, Venice is always ten degrees cooler—and that extends beyond the weather. Venice started as a resort town at the turn of the twentieth century—a bucolic, canal-lined send-up of its Italian counterpart dreamed up by developer Abbot Kinney. After the Second World War, artists moved there in droves.

Our clients lived on the idyllic walking streets in Venice, just a few blocks from those wonderful canals, and they were nearly done with their renovation when we came aboard. The pace of this job was staggeringly quick, and the clients were very willing to bend the rules established by their Craftsman-style home.

The main floor was intimately scaled, so the dining room, living room, and nook were essentially one space. Throwing that green velvet sofa on top of the striped kilim rug was a moment that just clicked. We had a lot of fun with our clients, and we were able to steer the project away from anything that felt too young. At the end of the day, the design was chic but inviting, and able to honor the cozy spirit of this seaside, Southern California cottage.

OPPOSITE The central hallway downstairs plays with scale and perspective and features a cheeky wallpaper by Deborah Bowness. FOLLOWING PAGES The main living room of the Craftsman cottage is bright and airy. The painted woodwork (considered a no-no in the classic Craftsman world) breathes new life into the space, with its NK modern sofa in a Donghia green velvet atop a vintage striped kilim.

PAGE 186 A close-up of the window perch in the living room, where Holland & Sherry wide wale corduroy covers a George Smith sofa.
PAGE 187 The dining room is part of the main living space, and we eased the edges of the clients' original table to help with the ergonomic flow of the room. OPPOSITE A classic period kitchen was re-created with a vintage stove. ABOVE NK Instagram. PG 190 The den is painted a moody gray to help contrast the bright white of the rest of the house. Again, the painted paneling helps modernize the traditional molding. PAGE 191 The cozy master bedroom features a dark Farrow & Ball wallpaper backdrop and natural linen NK headboard.

*The ache for home lives in all of us,
the safe place where we can go as we
are and not be questioned.*

— Maya Angelou

Santa Monica Mountains

Santa Monica Mountains

Past sleepy culs-de-sac and hundred-year-old oaks, this home at the base of the Santa Monica Mountains basks in a rare year-round glow. The structure was built as a hunting lodge, back when Los Angeles was still considered a prairie outpost, a wild frontier, a time when the wind swept through quiet towns and deer outnumbered people. This home had so many stories to tell, and drawing on that storied history, we sought to ignite the soul of the space while encouraging our imaginative clients to explore their own sense of whimsy, romance, and sophistication.

The original main room of the hunting lodge had vertical paneling, so we added similar panels through the main hallways as a gesture of solidarity with the past. We kept the brick floor in the kitchen because it worked beautifully as a humble material, just perfect for the casual feel we all hoped to rekindle. The living and dining rooms were combined to activate the space as a more communal, casual environment. Delft owl tiles line the fireplace, a quiet little mascot for the room.

The original dining room was transformed into a new style of Gaming Hall, complete with a grand taxidermy peacock that playfully hearkens back to the home's previous life, along with the family's personal collectibles displayed in antique cabinets.

Upstairs, the bedrooms and baths serve as the ultimate sanctuary. The master bathroom is a quiet portal into a time past that still looks forward. The clawfoot tub, botanical wallpaper, patinaed stone floors, and windows looking out to majestic pines make this a room for self-care and contemplation.

For us, history is a chance to tell a new story—a way to revive the romance of the past and spin some magic for the future. Together these elements create a space for a young family that enjoys a life that is both spontaneous and grounded, where the grand meets the quotidian, and nature is inspiration.

LEFT Original tongue-and-groove walls emphasize the entranceway. FOLLOWING PAGES Pale blue raffia wallpaper from Phillip Jeffries graces the living room walls, with a custom sofa covered in Liberty of London velvet.

LEFT Wallpaper by Marthe Armitage and vintage iron ship sconces adorn a powder room's walls. ABOVE Lightly whitewashed brick floors bring warmth into the bright, clean kitchen. FOLLOWING PAGES A narrow vestibule that had previously been used as a dining room morphed into a whimsical game room, with light fixtures by Jane Hallworth and artwork by Patricia Iglesias from the Sears-Peyton Gallery. The faux-taxidermy peacock, from JF Chen, is an homage to old halls in English country houses.

LEFT An enchanting master bath beckons with a custom pendant and vanity. The vintage Finnish wallpaper pattern contains deep blue and forest green, colors echoed by the fir trees just outside. ABOVE Custom dining chairs surround a vintage farm table in the bucolic breakfast room. FOLLOWING PAGES A vintage pendant from Obsolete, a custom credenza wrapped in Liberty of London fabric, and a rug by Beauvais combine to create a soothing master bedroom. PAGE 206 A custom wallpaper by Susan Harter in the home office creates a delightful surrounding landscape. PAGE 207 NK Shop vignette.

We are not the writers of our
clients' stories, but the editors.

— Nickey Kehoe

Malibu

Malibu

We rose early on a wet winter morning to greet the great Pacific Coast Highway on our way to Malibu. It was Saturday, so the sun decided to sleep in, and the marine layer hung heavy on the bluffs, like thick gray curtains. The house you see here is a traditional ranch house, built in the 1970s around the same time Bob Dylan and Neil Young were this beach town's most prominent residents.

Like a wandering ballad, the house seemed to go on forever as you ramble through the corridors. There was a formal, austere quality that our client wanted to enliven and shake up, so we were called in to bring light, modernity, and color into the space.

The challenge was to deformalize the space, and take out some of the starch, while still keeping it elegant and cool. This project has been ten years in the making and continues to shift and evolve. It's a wonderful quality to have in a client and home, the ability to grow with a family, to shift and change and see what the next Saturday has in store. And what a long, wonderful journey it's been.

OPPOSITE The blue of the formal dining room was inspired by an image of the house from *Architectural Digest* in the late 1980s, when the house was owned by Charles Bronson and Jill Ireland. PAGE 212 A focal point of the yellow den is a painting commissioned by Bronson when he built the house, which is intended to pay homage to the home's original site. Successive owners have left it with the house. PAGE 213 A photograph by Catherine Opie on an arresting, saturated blue wall.

ABOVE NK Instagram. OPPOSITE We painted the kitchen island a vibrant green and installed a custom pot rack. PAGE 216 Every surface of the formal living room was painted white by the previous owner. We discovered the marble fireplace upon removing the paint. The ceiling was sandblasted to reveal the Douglas fir timber. A metal mobile swirls above the room. PAGE 217 Henry the bulldog poses handsomely in the garden, one of many exterior lounging areas.

Toro Canyon

Toro Canyon

A second home is never secondary. This was our design philosophy for our clients and their young children in Summerland, California. Our working concept for the project was "Rancho-Swede," a balance of coastal equestrian with sophisticated Scandinavian *hygge*.

The husband is a pianist, and the wife is an avid horse rider. Accordingly, there's a lot of personal expression pulsing through this home. We always gather our best design inspiration from our clients, and here we found ways to weave their sense of whimsy and unfussy worldliness into something sophisticated and peaceful.

The library hosts a baby grand, plenty of books, and plenty of good conversation. The library was in fact the original living room, but our clients wanted it to be the place they hung out. The last time we visited, a puzzle was scattered on the coffee table along with open books and beanbag chairs.

The living room is the first thing you see when you come through the front door—it's almost an extended entryway. We selected a light and neutral palette to lead one's eyes out onto the Pacific Ocean. The ranch flair is most viscerally expressed through the fireplaces around the house, and the Monterey chairs in the family room.

The kids' bedroom is hands down one of our favorite designs, complete with wicker beds, Jennifer Shorto's Mini Cities wallpaper, and scalloped bookcases that spark absolute joy the minute you walk in. In the master bedroom, the clients fell in love with a Navajo-inspired fabric by BDDW, which we used on the headboard in another subtle nod to the ranch.

The rich colors are grounded by the abstract, modernist Beauvais rug, while the softest mustard velvet sofa and old trunks and branches collide for a bit of zesty fun. The clients surprised us by selecting a mauve color for their bathroom wainscoting. We'd suggested that color for a different use, but they loved it, and decided to bring it into the bathroom. Beauty and wonder can appear where you least expect them, but we find they often happen when two seemingly disparate ideas and moods are brought together. In Summerland, we complemented a seaside California ranch with Scandinavian accents and transformed an elegant dwelling into something cozy and spectacular.

OPPOSITE Palm trees, moss-covered brick, and dormant vines welcome our clients in all seasons.
FOLLOWING PAGES A vivid green paint called Ashland, from Portola Paints, adorns the walls of the library, which is a cozy, rich space where golden, camel, and berry tones mix and match in the upholstery.

*Perhaps home is not a place but
simply an irrevocable condition.*

— James Baldwin

PAGE 224 We repurposed a vintage radiator cover from Mexico as a console. PAGE 225 A chandelier from Woka hangs between sandblasted beams in this bright sunroom. LEFT His and hers Monterey chairs are the perfect nod to the vintage country California western aesthetic.

OPPOSITE Brass zodiac symbols line the vintage leather framed mirror.

ABOVE NK Instagram. Vintage ceramics as well as newer work by Rebekah Miles.

RIGHT A Josef Frank cabinet and vintage campaign chairs in the guest bedroom. PAGE 232 TOP The master bath is the perfect setting for a dreamy plunge while looking out to the Pacific Ocean. The deep forest green painted tub is from Waterworks; the French Sconces and vanity stool are vintage finds; and fireplace and shower are custom made. PAGE 232 BOTTOM A Waterworks vanity struck the right note of a rustic yet refined master bath. Vintage mirrors and rugs layer against the dusty rose painted bathroom. PAGE 233 A vintage-fabric-covered cabinet sits pretty below a jigsaw painting by Tyler Hayes. PAGES 234 235 Jennifer Shorto's Mini Cities wallpaper serves as a whimsical backdrop for the vintage rattan French beds.

Photography Credits

Acknowledgments

We would like to thank the Rizzoli team and Nic Taylor
of Thunderwing Studio for making this book come to life.

And to all of our friends, collaborators, and colleagues,
our work is not possible without you.

To our families (furry friends included), thank you for the
boundless support. We love you.

– Todd & Amy

First published in the United States of America in 2020 by
Rizzoli International Publications, Inc.
300 Park Avenue South, New York, NY 10010
www.rizzoliusa.com

Book Design: Thunderwing

Publisher: Charles Miers
Editor: Ron Broadhurst
Production Manager: Kaija Markoe
Managing Editor: Lynn Scrabis

Printed in Italy

2020 2021 2022 2023 2024 / 10 9 8 7 6 5 4 3 2 1

ISBN: 978-0-8478-6526-0
Library of Congress Control Number: 2020940375

Visit us online:
Facebook.com/RizzoliNewYork
Twitter: @Rizzoli_Books
Instagram.com/RizzoliBooks
Pinterest.com/RizzoliBooks
Youtube.com/user/RizzoliNY
Issuu.com/Rizzoli

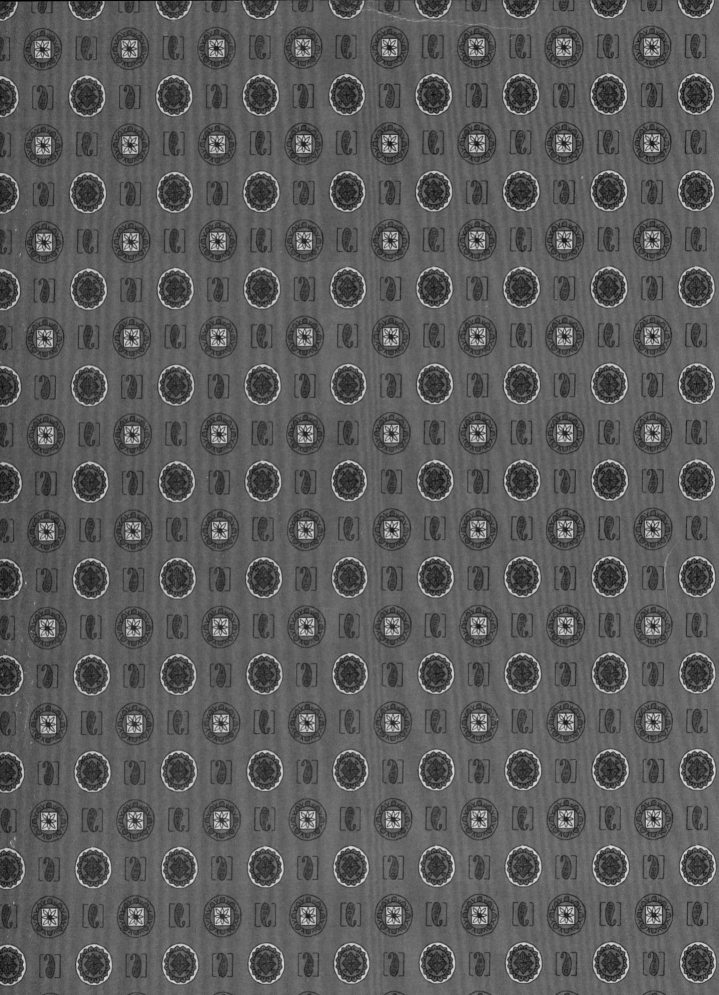